LET'S TELL TIME

Skill-Building Activities

by Jo E. Martin M. Ed.
and Diane Peregine

Edited by Judi Martschinke
Art coordination by Sue Smith
Cover by Rémy Simard

This book was previously printed
under the title *Let's Make Telling Time Easy.*

ISBN: 1-56911-713-6
© 1988 Learning Resources

Printed in the United States of America

TABLE OF CONTENTS

A NOTE FOR TEACHERS

So it's time to teach time. If you're wondering how to approach this often abstract and confusing concept with your first, second, or third graders, relax. We've developed a systematic approach for you. All you have to do is choose the activities that are appropriate for your students—and teach.

We begin by giving kids a brief background about time and the different methods people used to use to tell time. Always moving from the concrete to the abstract, many exercises relate time to children's lives—from what they do every day to the changes they notice in the seasons.

Telling time can be tough for those who don't know even the most basic information about clocks, so we've included activities that expose children to both analog and digital clocks and their parts. Because so many kids have only digital clocks in their homes, showing the similarities between analog and digital clocks is especially important.

Moving on, students are introduced to hours, minutes, and parts of hours. Throughout, children are challenged with games and exercises that use their bodies, stretch their minds, and test their understanding. So turn the page, and let the fun begin!

NOTE: Text that is set in this style is meant for the instructor.

Text that is set in this style is meant for the student.

A NOTE FOR TEACHERS

Begin a discussion about time by asking students how they know whether it is day or night, Monday or Saturday, January or July, or spring or winter. Next, write the following sentences on the chalkboard. Read them with children and ask students to use the context clues in each sentence to tell what the underlined words mean. Then ask children to listen as you read aloud the story Time.

---

1. In gym, Bob runs around the track, does ten sit-ups, and then rests. He repeats the same cycle everyday. *(A series of events that happen in the same order over and over.)*
2. Janetta thinks the new moon looks like a skinny, shining banana hanging in the sky. *(The phase of the moon when it is invisible or has a barely visible cresent shape.)*
3. The full moon is so big and round it looks like it could bounce across the sky. *(The phase of the moon when it has a completely round shape.)*
4. At the start of each new month, the calendar is flipped to the next page. *(Something that keeps track of days, months, and years.)*

TIME

Early people needed to keep track of time so that they would know when to plant seeds or when to celebrate special days. They knew that every morning the sun rose and every night it set, so they began to keep track of days by counting each time the sun rose. Next, they watched the moon. They noticed that the sun rose about 30 times from when the moon was full to when it was full again. Based on the cycles of the sun and the moon, ancient people set up a calendar that had 12 months and 354 days. They also watched plants and animals to learn when the seasons changed. Nature changes at the same time every year, and there is a cycle for when plants and animals need to grow and when they need to rest.

Egyptians noticed that the stars moved across the night sky in a regular pattern, so they set up their calendar around the bright star named *Sirius*. Sirius would appear once every 365 days, and each time it reappeared the Egyptians began a new year.

The Mayan Indians studied the sun, moon and stars. They divided their year into 18 months, with 20 days in each month. To these 360 days, the Mayans added 5 bad luck days to make up a year of 365 days.

The calendar we use today is a lot like the one the Romans used. They named each month and added one extra day to February every four years. We still do this, and when February has an extra day we call it *Leap Year*.

Today we use a calendar designed by Pope Gregory XIII in 1582. It has 12 months and 365 days. Some months have 30 days (April, June, September, and November); the rest have 31 days. An exception is February, which has 28 days except when it is Leap Year—then it has 29 days. Each day has 24 hours.

Activity: To emphasize the concept that time is sequential and cyclical, ask children to draw cartoons of themselves at morning, noon and nighttime, or to draw the four seasons.

CHOOSE THE SEASON

1. Color green all of the things that are found in *spring*.
2. Draw a blue circle around all of the things found in *summer*.
3. Use orange to color all of the things that are found in *autumn*.
4. Draw a red X through all of the things found in *winter*.

6

A YEAR

Below are pictures of Bob from the family photo album.
Draw a line from each picture to the correct description.

1. Bob at 1 year old.
   Isn't he cute?

2. Bob's first day of school.
   He's 5 years old.

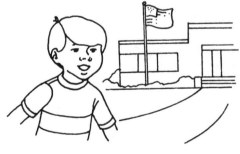

3. Bob, 25 years old,
   on his wedding day.

4. Bob at 70 years old with
   his grandson.

7

THE MONTH

There are 12 months in a year. Each month is about 4 weeks long. The number of days in a month changes from month to month. A good way to remember the names of the months and the number of days in each is to memorize this saying: "Thirty days has September, April, June and November. All the rest have 31, except February which has 28 and in Leap Year has 29."

Cut out the cards below and poke holes through the dots. Pull short pieces of yarn through the dots to connect the cards. Form a time line of 12 months such as the example below. Under each month hang pictures of important dates that occur during that month.

| JANUARY | FEBRUARY | MARCH | APRIL | MAY | JUNE | JULY | AUGUST | SEPTEMBER | OCTOBER | NOVEMBER | DECEMBER |

○ **JANUARY** ○	○ **FEBRUARY** ○
○ **MARCH** ○	○ **APRIL** ○
○ **MAY** ○	○ **JUNE** ○
○ **JULY** ○	○ **AUGUST** ○
○ **SEPTEMBER** ○	○ **OCTOBER** ○
○ **NOVEMBER** ○	○ **DECEMBER** ○

THE CALENDAR

A calendar is a chart of a year.
It shows the days of the week, the weeks, the month, and important dates. There are many kinds of calendars—some hang, some sit on desks, some fit into your pocket—but they all tell you similar things.

1. **Look at different calendars. What does each one tell you?**

2. **Fill in this calendar with the month of your birthday. Write the month, the days, and the numbers in the appropriate places. Then decorate your birthday square.**

THE WEEK

A week is now seven days long. It was not always that way. The Greeks had a 10 day week; the Soviet Union tried to use five and six day weeks.

Seven days was the best way to divide up weeks because that is how long it takes for the moon to travel through each of its phases.

In our country most workers look forward to the *weekend*, when they do not have to go to work or school and they may spend Saturday and Sunday as they choose.

---

1. Cut out the names of the days of the week below and put them in order.

WEDNESDAY	**TUESDAY**
THURSDAY	**SATURDAY**
MONDAY	**FRIDAY**
SUNDAY	

2. Cut pictures from a magazine of people doing different things. Arrange the pictures under the name of the day on which you think the activity is happening. (For example, a picture of people attending church could go under SUNDAY; Thanksgiving Dinner would go under THURSDAY; children playing basketball might go under whatever day your class has gym.)

3. Draw a picture of your favorite thing to do on a *weekend*.

SEASONS

Nature has its own way of marking the passage of time throughout the year. The four seasons—spring, summer, autumn, and winter—make up a year in nature.

Spring is the time when animals come out of a deep sleep called *hibernation* and give birth; when plants begin to grow, and when the weather becomes warm.

Summer marks the time when fruits ripen and the weather becomes hot.

In autumn, animals begin storing food for winter, leaves change color and fall off the trees, and the temperature turns cool.

Many animals and plants sleep through winter's cold temperatures and snows.

In spring, nature begins a new year.

Color these symbols of each season. Write the name of each season under the symbol.

11

THE BEGINNING OF THE DAY

Put these pictures in order by writing 1 below the drawing of the activity that happens first, and 2 below the drawing of the activity that happens second, and so on.

FIRST THINGS FIRST

Put these pictures in order by writing 1 below the drawing of the activity that happens first, 2 below the drawing of the activity that happens second, and so on.

_____

_____

_____

_____

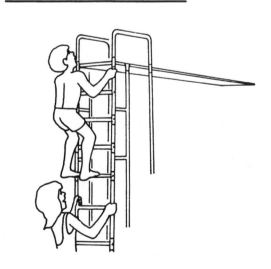

_____

_____

THE DAY

Keeping track of days was the first way people used to tell time. Events were described as happening either *that day* or *before* that day. As people needed to communicate things that were going to happen, the *future* was described.

To most people, their day is still the time between when they wake up until they go to bed. A day really begins when most people are asleep and continues for 24 hours. We say that the new day begins at midnight — the same time the old day ends.

1. **Explain what *yesterday* and *tomorrow* mean. Then make a list of things you did yesterday and things you will do tomorrow.**
2. **Make a book of *Special Days.* Be sure to include your birthday and holidays.**
3. **Draw a picture of what an earth day would look like to someone in space.**

IT'S ALL IN A DAY

Put these pictures in order by writing 1 under what happens first, 2 under what happens second, and so on.

NIGHT AND DAY

Cut apart the strips on the bottom of the page and paste them on the correct side.

LIGHT	DARK

---

1 o'clock in the morning	4 o'clock in the afternoon
10 o'clock in the morning	10 o'clock at night
12 midnight	11 o'clock at night
2 o'clock in the morning	12 noon
4 o'clock in the morning	2 o'clock in the afternoon

THINGS I DO DURING THE DAY

Make a book titled _Things I Do During the Day_ to show what your day is like. To make a book, fold two pieces of paper in half. Put one paper inside the other and staple them together at the fold. Write the title on the cover. Then cut out the following sentences and glue them to the bottom of the pages. Draw a picture that shows what each sentence says.

This is what I do between breakfast and school time.

This is what I do in school before lunch.

This is a picture of what I do for lunch.

This is what I do in school after lunch.

These are some things I do before bedtime.

TRAVELING AROUND THE CLOCK

Each day has 24 hours in it. These 24 hours are split into two parts, with each part having 12 hours in it.

The first 12 hours start at 12 o'clock, midnight, and end at 12 o'clock, noon. We call these hours the A.M. or *morning* hours.

The second 12 hours begin at 12 o'clock, noon, and end at 12 o'clock, midnight. These hours are called the P.M. hours and they happen in the *afternoon, evening,* and *night.*

Morning or *A.M.* times, are written like this:

     3:00 A.M.

Afternoon, evening, and *night* times, or *P.M.* times, are written like this:

     3:00 P.M.

In each box, color the pictures of those objects that you would most likely use at the time shown.

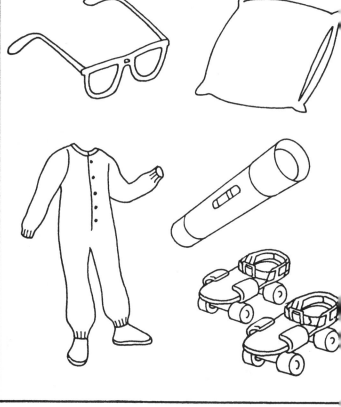

11:00 A.M.   11:00 P.M.

MORNING AND NIGHT

Look at the times listed below. If the time shows a *morning* hour, color the sun next to it. If the time shows an *afternoon,* *evening,* or *nighttime* hour, color the star next to it.

6:00 P.M.

7:00 A.M.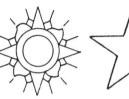

0:00 A.M.

4:00 P.M.

9:00 A.M.

5:00 A.M.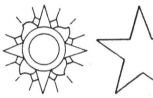

2:00 P.M.

1:00 P.M.

1:00 A.M.

10:00 P.M.

19

NOON AND MIDNIGHT

Twelve o'clock is a special time. It is neither A.M. nor P.M. The 12:00 that occurs at night is called *midnight* and the 12:00 that occurs during the day is called *noon*.

Midnight means *middle of the night*. Many years ago, people thought that midnight was halfway between the time the sun set and the time the sun rose the next day.

People used to think that *noon* was when the sun was straight above them and there were no shadows.

Here is how you can see how well the sun tells time:

Go outdoors with a friend a little before noon. Ask your friend to stand straight in the sunlight. Does your friend have a shadow? When the shadow is so small that it is under your friend's feet, it is exactly noon according to the sun.

A.M. AND P.M.

1. **Read the items on the A.M. and P.M. sides of the chart. Draw a line through any item that does not belong on the side where it is listed.**

A.M.   P.M.

A.M.	P.M.
eat breakfast	put on pajamas
get dressed	have a bedtime snack
do homework	go to school
watch the stars	set the table for supper
ride the bus home	do homework
say "Good Morning"	make your bed
watch fireworks	wake up

2. **Think of things you do in the morning, afternoon, evening, and night and add them to each side of the chart.**

MEASURING TIME

Any sound or movement that repeats itself can be used to measure time. Working with a friend, follow each direction below to measure time.

1. How many blocks can you stack while a friend sings "Mary Had a Little Lamb" one time? _____

2. How many times can you tap your foot while a friend writes his or her name on the chalkboard? _____

3. How many times can you blink your eyes while a friend says the alphabet? _____

4. How many times can you bounce a ball while a friend ties his or her shoes? _____

5. How many times does your heart beat while a friend eats a cracker? (To feel your heartbeat, or *pulse*, put your fingers gently against the side of your neck.) _____

6. How many times can you jump rope while your friend sings "Happy Birthday?" _____

7. How many times can you clap your hands while your friend says the days of the week? _____

A NOTE FOR TEACHERS

Teachers:

Share this brief history of timekeepers with students. If possible, it would be helpful to have samples or pictures of some of the timepieces described for children to examine. Directions for children to make water clocks and sand timers follow.

TIMEKEEPERS

A long time ago, people did not have the kinds of clocks and watches we use today. One of the earliest ways people had to tell time was to watch the position of the sun and the length of the shadows it made. Babylonians and Egyptians used **shadow clocks** thousands of years ago. **Sundials** are a form of shadow clock that can still be found today. They work by having a rod that points to the north or south pole. As the sun moves across the sky from east to west, the rod makes a shadow on a dial with markings that show the time.

The problem with shadow clocks is that whenever the sun does not shine, such as at night or on rainy days, no shadows are made and they cannot be used. To solve this problem, the Egyptians used water clocks called **clepsydras.** These clocks looked like large bowls with markings inside and a hole in the bottom. Once they were filled with water, the water would run out the bottom and the markings would show the time. But there were also problems with clepsydras. The water often was spilled when the clocks were moved, and in places where the temperature got cold enough the water would freeze.

Sand timers did not have the problems that shadow clocks and clepsydras had. No one knows who invented sand timers first, but they were used until the middle of the 1600s. A sand timer is usually made of glass. It has two parts that can hold sand and these parts are connected by a small opening. When all the sand is in one part, it is turned over so that the sand has to squeeze through the opening into the bottom part. The amount of sand that falls into the bottom portion tells how much time has passed. The **egg timers** people still use today which tell when an egg is cooked are tiny forms of sand timers.

Eventually, other types of time keepers were invented. **Cuckoo clocks** and **grandfather clocks** work when a weight drops down to move gears. The gears make a pointer move to show the time. **Pendulum clocks** have a weight that swings back and forth to keep time. Some clocks and watches have a spring inside them that is wound up. Today, many clocks and watches run on electricity, batteries, or crystals.

QUESTIONS

1. What was the earliest way people had to tell time? (*They would watch the sun and the length of shadows it made.*)

2. If you lived a long time ago in a very cold place, why would you not use a water clock, or clepsydra, to tell time? (*because the water would freeze*)

3. Why do you think sand is used in egg timers? (*because the grains are so small they can easily pass through the hole*)

3. How does a pendulum clock work? (*A weight swings back and forth.*)

5. How do many clocks and watches work today? (*They run on electricity, batteries, or crystals.*)

MAKE A WATER CLOCK

Students will need:

> a paper cup with a pinhole
> a small glass
> a strip of masking tape
> a black pen
> enough water to fill the paper cup

Ask students to put the strip of masking tape vertically on the side of the glass. Next, distribute the paper cups with pinholes for students to place in the tops of their glasses. Tell children that once they fill their cups with water, you will tell them every time two minutes have passed so that they can draw a line on the tape to mark how high the water is. Ask the students to fill their cups at the same time, then call out two-minute intervals until most students have had all the water run out of their cups. Then have children pour out the water and use their clocks to time the following activities.

1. **How many times can you jump up and down in two minutes?**

2. **How many times can you say the alphabet in four minutes?**

3. **How many math problems can you do in six minutes?**

4. **How many pages can you read in your favorite book in eight minutes?**

READINESS ACTIVITIES FOR TELLING TIME

1. Introduce Children to Analog and Digital Clocks

At home, children often encounter only digital clocks. To help them understand the relationship between digital and analog clock faces, place a digital clock under the analog clock in your classroom several weeks before you begin the study of time. Make sure the clocks are synchronized. As often as possible, call children's attention to the clocks when it is time for a change in activities. For example, "At 12 o'clock we will go to lunch. That's only five minutes away;" "I see that it is 2 o'clock so we must go to gym."

2. Develop the Concept of "One Minute"

Young children many times do not have an understanding of different lengths of time. To help them become aware of how long a minute is, play the following game when you have free time. Ask students to close their eyes and put their heads down on their desks. Challenge them to raise their hands when they think one minute has passed. If students' estimates vary greatly, have them put their heads down once again and this time you tell them when one minute is up. Then repeat the game to see if children's guesses more closely match the passage of one minute.

Have students work individually or in groups to list things they think they can do in one minute, such as brush their teeth or drink a glass of water. If possible, have students perform some of these activities as you time them to see if they guessed correctly.

3. Develop the Concept of "One Hour"

This activity will acquaint children with the difference between one minute and one hour. When your classroom clocks are "on the hour," ask children to glance at them. Then set a timer for one hour. When the timer goes off, have students note the new time on the clocks. Ask children to list all the things they did from the time they first looked at the clocks to when the timer went off one hour later. Have them tell whether they think they could do all those things in one minute and explain their answers. Last, set the timer for one minute as children continue to work to emphasize the difference between one minute and one hour.

4. Have Children Estimate Time on Tasks

Try this exercise to help children become aware of the relationship between time and what they do in their everyday lives. Before beginning various tasks, have students guess how long they think it will take to complete each task, such as walking to music class, cleaning the room, drawing a picture, and tying shoes. Write their estimates on the board. Time each task and note the times next to the estimates for children to compare.

5. Develop an Understanding of "Clockwise"

Most children do not understand what direction "clockwise" is. To develop visual and kinesthetic awareness, draw a large round clockface on the board. Use an arrow to show which way the hands move around the clock. Then face the clock with your back to the class and move your arm in a clockwise motion, starting and ending at 12 o'clock. Ask students to stand and face the board as you each move an arm in a clockwise direction together. Repeat several times.

THE HUMAN CLOCK

The following activity will provide children with a concrete experience for telling time.

1. Preparation

Using lightly colored 8½-by-11-inch construction paper, write the numerals 1 through 12 with one numeral on each sheet. Cut 2 clock hands from black posterboard—one minute hand (long and thin; 36-by-4 inches) and one hour hand (short and fat; 18-by-6-inches).

2. Make the Clock Face

Ask 12 volunteers to be numeral holders and give each child one numeral card. Have the numeral holders stand in numerical order, then form a circle. Make sure that the 12 is across from the 6, the 3 is across from the 9 and so on.

3. Form the Clock Hands

Ask 2 more volunteers to be the clock hands. Give one child the minute hand and have him or her stand in the center of the circle and point the hand at the 12. Explain that there are 60 minutes in every hour and that every time the minute hand goes all the way around the clock 60 minutes have passed.

Instruct the minute-hand-holder to slowly turn clockwise around the circle as the class counts to 60. Make sure he or she once again points to the 12 at the end of the exercise.

Next, invite the hour-hand-holder to also stand in the center of the circle and point to the 1. Explain that the hour hand always shows what hour the clock is telling about. Ask what hour the clock will tell about if the hour hand is point to the 1 (*1 o'clock*). Have the hour-hand-holder turn clockwise and point to each numeral as the children say the numerals. Remind students taht there are 12 A.M. hours and 12 P.M. hours, and that is why the clock has 12 numerals on it.

4. Telling Time

Ask the minute-hand-holder to continue pointing to the 12 and the hour-hand-holder to point to the 1. Tell children that because the hour hand is pointing to the 1 and the minute hand has not moved away from the 12, the time shown is 1 o'clock. Write *1 o'clock* on the board.

Continue having the minute-hand-holder point to the 12. Ask a new volunteer to point the hour hand at the 2. Have children tell what time the clock is showing (*2 o'clock*). Repeat the procedure for the remaining 10 hours, giving as many children as possible turns. Save the clock parts for use with an activity on page 35.

5. Questions

How many minutes are in one hour? (*60*)

How many A.M. hours are there in a day? (*12*)

How many P.M. hours are there in a day? (*12*)

What does the minute hand show? (*how many minutes have passed*)

What does the hour hand show? (*which hour the clock is telling about*)

BUILD A CLOCK

1. Fill in the numerals around the clock face. 12 goes at the top.

2. Color the minute hand red and the hour hand green. Look at the difference in their lengths. The minute hand is always longer than the hour hand.

3. Cut out the clock hands and fasten them to the center of the clock face with a metal connector. *Save this clock for other activities.*

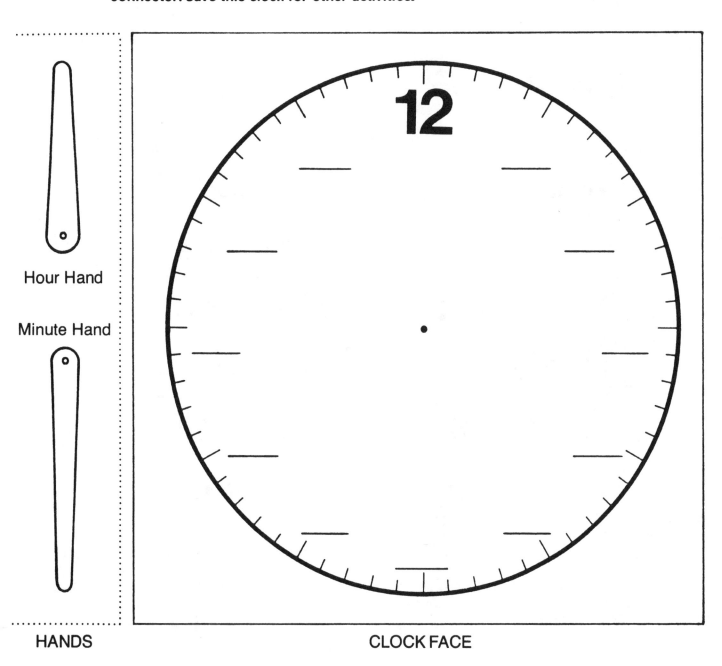

Hour Hand

Minute Hand

HANDS

CLOCK FACE

SHOW A TIME

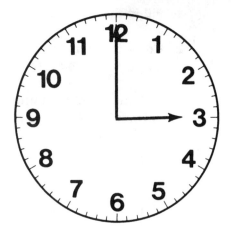

Cut apart the time slips to the right and fold each in half.

Pick a time slip from the group and set that time on your own clock face.

Save your time slips for another activity.

For example, the clock face shows 3 o'clock. Can you explain why?

TIME SLIPS

12 o'clock	**2 o'clock**
1 o'clock	**5 o'clock**
7 o'clock	**6 o'clock**
4 o'clock	**9 o'clock**
3 o'clock	**11 o'clock**
8 o'clock	**10 o'clock**

Your teacher may write a time on the board and ask you to show that time on your clock face.

Work with a partner. Take turns picking a time slip, then one of you show the time on your clock face as the other person says the time.

DRAW TIME ON A CLOCK FACE

On the clock faces below, draw the times given on the time slips you saved. The minute hands are already drawn in. Then write the times on the lines under the clock faces.

1. _____ o'clock

2. _____ o'clock

3. _____ o'clock

4. _____ o'clock

5. _____ o'clock

6. _____ o'clock

7. _____ o'clock

8. _____ o'clock

9. _____ o'clock

10. _____ o'clock

11. _____ o'clock

12. _____ o'clock

MATCH THE TIMES

There are different ways to write times. One way is to write the word *o'clock* after the numeral, such as *2 o'clock*. Another way to write 2 o'clock is 2:00. This is the way digital clocks show time. The first numeral or numerals show what hour the clock is telling about, like the hour hand on a round clock face. In this example the hour both clocks are telling about is 2. The numerals shown after the colon (:) tell how many minutes have passed, like the minute hand on a round clock face. Since our example shows 00, that means no minutes have passed and it is exactly 2 o'clock.

Write the times shown on the round clock faces, then match them to the digital clock faces.

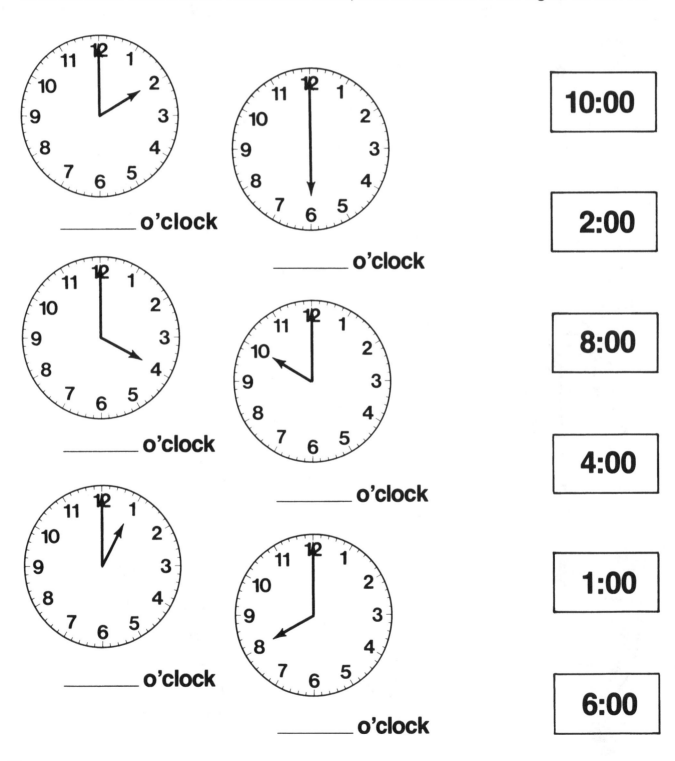

_____ o'clock

_____ o'clock

_____ o'clock

_____ o'clock

_____ o'clock

_____ o'clock

10:00

2:00

8:00

4:00

1:00

6:00

CLOCK PUZZLES

Cut out the pieces and mix them up. Then match each clock face to the correct time.

5 o'clock

1 o'clock

9:00

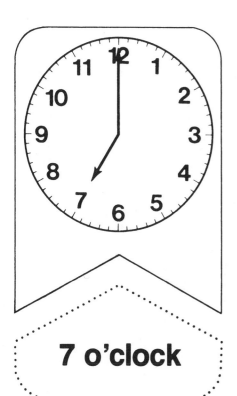
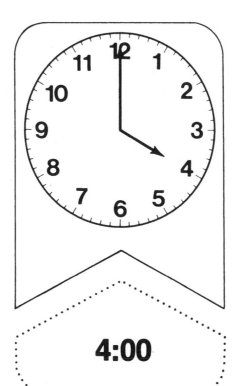
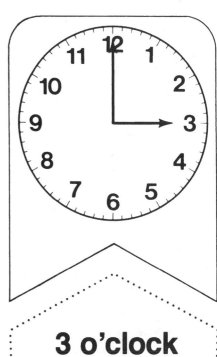

7 o'clock

4:00

3 o'clock

MORE CLOCK PUZZLES

Cut out the pieces and mix them up. Then match each clock face to the correct time.

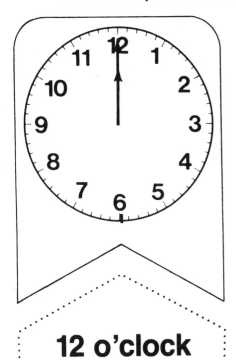

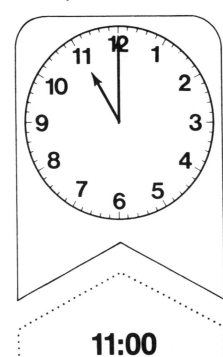

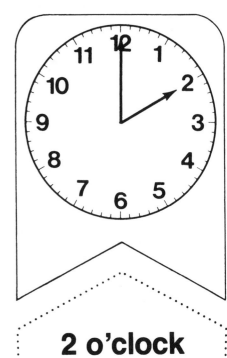

12 o'clock

11:00

2 o'clock

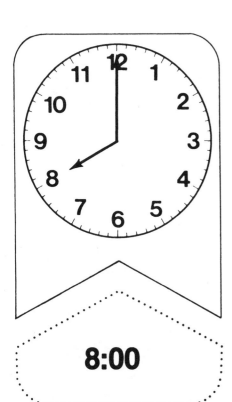

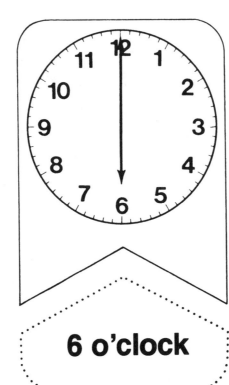

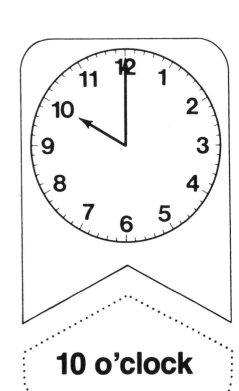

8:00

6 o'clock

10 o'clock

32

HOW MANY HOURS ARE YOU AWAKE?

Every day for one week, write down the time you get up and the time you go to bed on the chart below.

	Time You Got Up	Time You Went To Bed
Monday	_____	_____
Tuesday	_____	_____
Wednesday	_____	_____
Thursday	_____	_____
Friday	_____	_____
Saturday	_____	_____
Sunday	_____	_____

Find out how many hours you were awake each day. First, count the hours from the time you got up until noon. If you got up at 7:00 A.M., you were up 5 hours until noon. Then count the hours from noon until you went to bed. If you went to bed at 8:00 P.M., you were up another 8 hours. Add your A.M. and P.M. hours together to find out the number of hours you were awake. In this example, 5 A.M. hours and 8 P.M. hours equal 13 hours awake. Fill in the amount of hours you were awake each day on the bar graph below.

Hours
Awake

	Monday	Tuesday	Wednesday	Thursday	Friday	Saturday	Sunday
18							
17							
16							
15							
14							
13							
12							
11							
10							

WORD PROBLEMS

Use your clock face to help you answer the word problems below.

1. Anna is playing but she must begin her homework at 4:00 P.M. It is now 2:00 P.M. How many more hours can Anna play?

_____

2. Michael and Jason want to build a fort in the backyard. If they start building at 10:00 A.M. and finish at 3:00 P.M., how many hours will the fort take to build?

_____

3. Tina's mom called to say she will be home in one hour. It is now 5:00 P.M. What time will it be when Tina's mom gets home?

_____

4. Pat went to Jan's birthday party at 1:00 P.M. The party lasted 3 hours. What time was it when Pat left the party?

_____

5. Sean spent four hours at the amusement park. He got to the park at 1:00 P.M. What time was it when he left?

_____

6. Diane wants to see a movie that begins at 6:00 P.M. It is now 11:00 A.M. In how many hours will the movie start?

_____

COUNT THE MINUTES

Remember that there are 60 minutes in one hour. When the minute hand moves from line to line on this clock face, it shows the minutes passing. Each time it moves from one line to the next, it means one minute has passed.

If there are 60 minutes in one hour, how many lines do you think there are on this clock face? Check your guess by writing the minutes of an hour, from 1 to 60, above these lines. The counting has already been started for you.

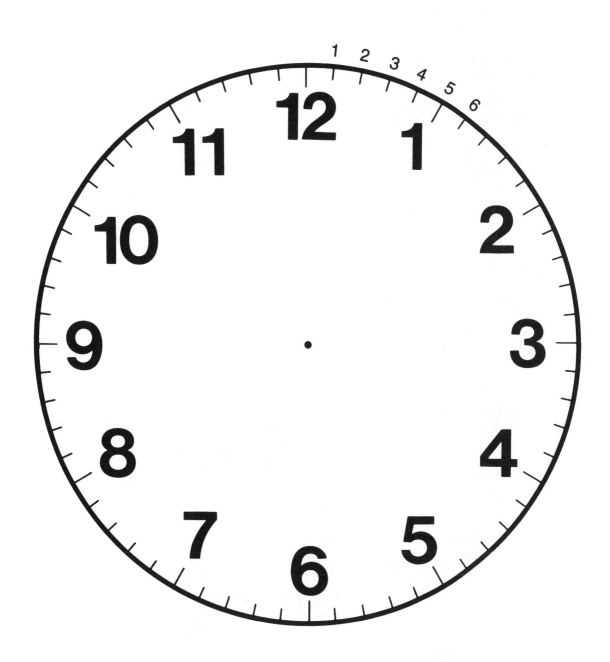

THE HUMAN CLOCK
HALF PAST THE HOUR

1. Use the clock pieces made for the activity on page 26 to have children once again form a human clock. Use volunteers to review telling time "on the hour."

2. Ask the child holding the minute hand to point it at the 12. Have the minute-hand-holder turn clockwise so that he or she ends up pointing the hand at the 6. Explain that when the minute hand points to the 6 it has gone halfway around the clock, so we say it is "half past" the hour. Ask: "If there are 60 minutes in one hour, how many minutes are there in half an hour?" (30) "How many minutes have passed when the minute hand points to the 6?" (30)

3. Tell children that when the minute hand moves, the hour hand also moves a little bit. For example, at three-thirty the hour hand is between the 3 and the 4.

4. Have children practice a variety of "half past" times. Make sure the hour-hand-holder points the hand between the numerals involved.

5. Give as many students as possible chances to be part of the human clock. Then say several "half past" times aloud for children to show on their individual clock faces.

   Example: At half past 4 the child holding the minute hand points the hand at the 6, while the child holding the hour hand points that hand between the 4 and the 5.

HALF HOURS

One hour can be divided into two equal parts. Each of these parts is called a *half*. When two halves are put together they equal one hour.

One hour has 60 minutes in it. Each half hour has 30 minutes in it. When two half hours are put together they equal one hour that has 60 minutes in it.

Look at the clock face below. The dotted line divides it into two halves. On each part, trace the words "one half."

Now cut out the clock face and divide it into two halves by cutting along the dotted line. Color each half a different color. Then put the halves back together to equal one hour.

QUESTIONS

1. How many minutes are in one hour? _____

2. How many minutes are in one half hour? _____

3. How many halves are in one hour? _____

4. If two halves are put together to make one hour, how many minutes will the hour have? _____

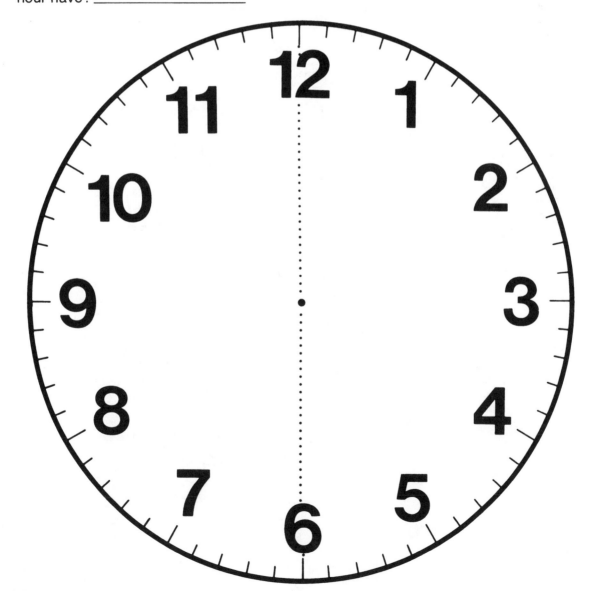

37

HALF PAST THE HOUR

Photocopy and distribute page 39 to the children. Ask students to look at the minute hand on the example that illustrates 2 o'clock. State that the minute hand is pointing to the 12 because it has not started moving to show minutes passing. Explain that since the hour hand is pointing to the 2 and the minute hand has not moved away from its starting point at the 12, the time is 2 o'clock.

Ask students how many minutes are in one hour. (*60*) Then have them tell what half of 60 minutes equals. (*30 minutes*) Instruct students to look at the half-past-2 example. Remind the class that each line on the clock represents one minute. Because there are 60 minutes in every hour, there are 60 lines on the clock. Ask students how many lines they think there are on half the clock if they know that 30 minutes is half of 60 minutes. (*30 minutes*) Have them check their guesses by counting the lines, starting with the lines immediately following the 12, up to and including the 6.

Next, have students look at where the minute hand is on the half-past-2 clock face. State that when the minute hand moves halfway around the clock it points to the 6. When this happens, we say the time is *half past* whatever hour the hour hand is telling about.

Ask children to remember that as the minute hand moves, the hour hand also moves toward the next numeral. Explain that in this example the minute hand is pointing to the 6 and the hour is moving away from the 2 toward the 3, so the time is *half past 2*. As the minute hand shows more minutes passing, the hour hand moves closer to the next numeral.

Do the first exercise with the children, modeling and looking at the positions of the minute and hour hands. Have children complete the remaining exercises independently.

HALF PAST THE HOUR

2 o'clock

half past 2

Fill in the blanks to show the time on each clock face below.

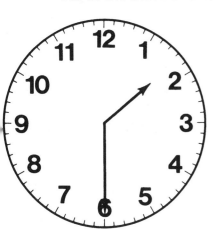

half past _____

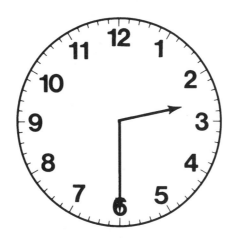

half past _____

half past _____

half past _____

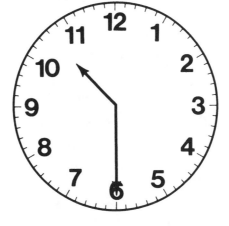

half past _____

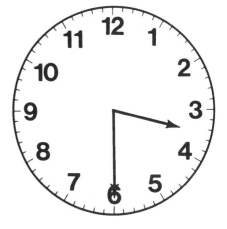

half past _____

MATCH THE TIMES

Draw a line from each clock face to its matching time.

half past one

half past eleven

half past eight

half past ten

half past two

half past four

half past six

half past nine

half past seven

half past three

ANOTHER WAY TO WRITE HALF PAST THE HOUR

Half past 4 can also be written as 4:30.

This hand tells
how many minutes
of the hour
have passed.

This hand shows
the hour the
clock is telling
about.

half past 4   **4:30**

This digital clock face shows the same time as the clock face on the left.

This numeral shows the
hour the clock is telling about.

These numerals tell
how many minutes of
the hour have passed.

4:30

Look at the minute hands on the round clock faces below. Under each one, write the same number of minutes passed on the digital clock faces. Remember that half past any hour is 30 minutes after that hour.

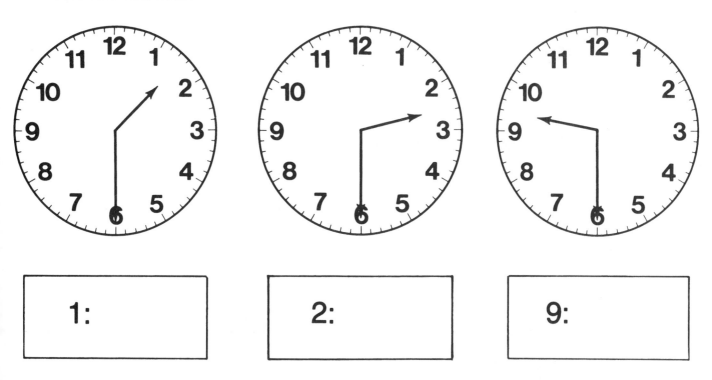

| 1: | 2: | 9: |

MATCH THE TIMES

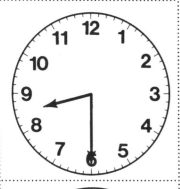

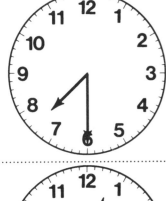

Cut out each of the clock faces below. Paste each clock face in the space that shows the same time.

half past 8
or
8:30

half past 12
or
12:30

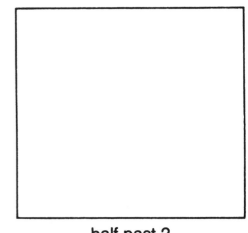

half past 2
or
2:30

half past 7
or
7:30

half past 6
or
6:30

SHOW A TIME

Cut apart the time slips to the right and fold each in half.

Pick a time slip from the group and set that time on your own clock face. Save your time slips for another activity.

For example, the clock face below shows half past 12, or 12:30. Can you explain why?

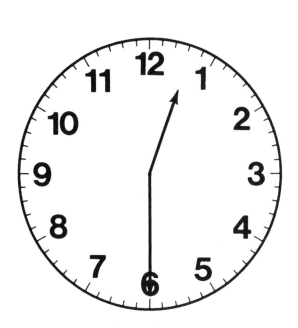

TIME SLIPS

half past 3 or 3:30	half past 7 or 7:30
half past 1 or 1:30	half past 8 or 8:30
half past 4 or 4:30	half past 6 or 6:30
half past 10 or 10:30	half past 12 or 12:30
half past 2 or 2:30	half past 9 or 9:30
half past 11 or 11:30	half past 5 or 5:30

Your teacher may write a time on the board and ask you to show that time on your clock face.

Work with a partner. Take turns picking a time slip, then one of you show the time on your clock face as the other person says the time.

DRAW TIME ON A CLOCK FACE

On the clock faces below, draw the times given on the time slips you saved.
Then write the times under the clock faces.

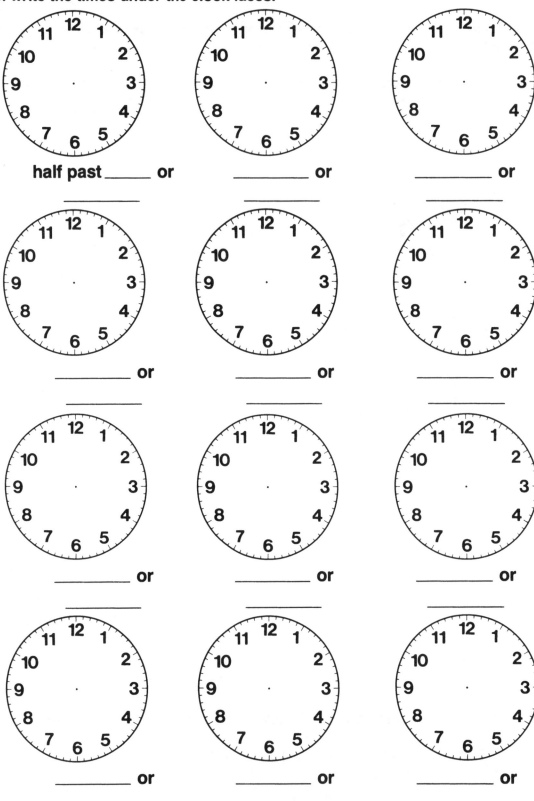

half past _____ or

_____ or

_____ or

_____ or

_____ or

_____ or

_____ or

_____ or

_____ or

_____ or

_____ or

_____ or

QUARTER HOURS

You already know that one hour can be divided into two equal parts. Each of these parts is called a half. When two halves are put together they equal one hour.

One hour can also be divided into four equal parts. Each of these parts is called a *quarter*. There are 15 minutes in one quarter of an hour. When four quarter hours are put together they equal one hour that has 60 minutes in it.

Look at the clock face below. The dotted lines divide it into four quarters. On each part, trace the words "one quarter."

Now cut out the clock face and divide it into four quarters by cutting along the dotted lines. Color each quarter a different color. Then put the quarters back together to equal one hour.

QUESTIONS

1. How many mintues are in one hour? _____

2. How many minutes are in one quarter of an hour? _____

3. How many quarters are in one hour? _____

4. If four quarters are put together to make one hour,
   how many minutes will the hour have? _____

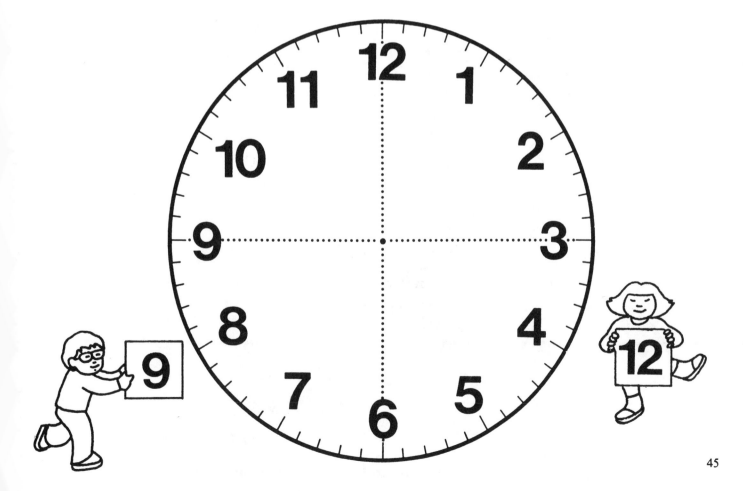

DRAW QUARTER HOURS

When one quarter of an hour has passed, we can say the time as either a *quarter after* the hour or a *quarter past* the hour. The clock face below is an example.

When there is only one quarter of an hour left before the next hour, we can say the time as either a *quarter before* the next hour or a *quarter to* the next hour. The clock face below is an example.

Draw the hands on the clock faces below to show the times written under them. Remember that the more minutes the minute hand shows passing, the closer the hour hand gets to the next numeral.

quarter after 1
or
quarter past 1

quarter before 10
or
quarter to 10

quarter after 6

quarter past 3

quarter after 9

quarter before 4

quarter to 11

quarter before 7

quarter after 8

quarter to 5

quarter past 12

46

COUNTING BY FIVES

LEARNING RESOURCES

When telling time, minutes are often rounded off to the nearest five minutes. Help students strengthen their counting skills by repeating the following activities until they demonstrate a clear understanding of counting by fives.

ACTIVITIES

1. Form a line of 20 counters. Ask students to silently count along with you as you point to each of the first four counters. When you point to the fifth counter, say "five." Continue in the same manner until the twentieth counter is reached. For example:

   silent silent silent silent **five,** s s s s **ten,** s s s s **fifteen,** s s s s **twenty**

2. Remind students that every hour has 60 minutes. Then play a clap and shout game to practice counting by fives to 60.

Model patting your thighs in rhythm four times and then clapping your hands once as you simultaneously shout "five." Keep the rhythm going, patting your thighs four more times then clapping as you shout "ten." Explain that when you pat your thighs you are silently counting the numbers between five, ten, and so on. Ask children to play the game with you.

3. This exercise provides additional practice for counting by fives to 60. Divide the class into two sides and line up the children so that the sides face each other. The first child on one side begins by saying "five." Then the first child on the opposite side says "ten." Continue alternating sides until a count of 60 is made. If a student makes an error, classmates may volunteer help to figure out the correct answer. Resume the exercise and repeat as often as necessary to give every child a chance to respond.

COUNT THE MINUTES

When counting the minutes in an hour by fives, remember that there are 60 minutes in one hour. Each time the minute hand reaches another numeral on a clock face, it means another five minutes have passed. A digital clock does not have a minute hand, so it just tells you how many minutes have passed in the place where minutes are shown.

Count the minutes in one hour by putting your finger on each numeral on the clock face below as you move clockwise around it counting by fives. Then write the correct number of minutes next to each numeral that tells how many minutes have passed when the minute hand reaches that point. The counting has already been started for you.

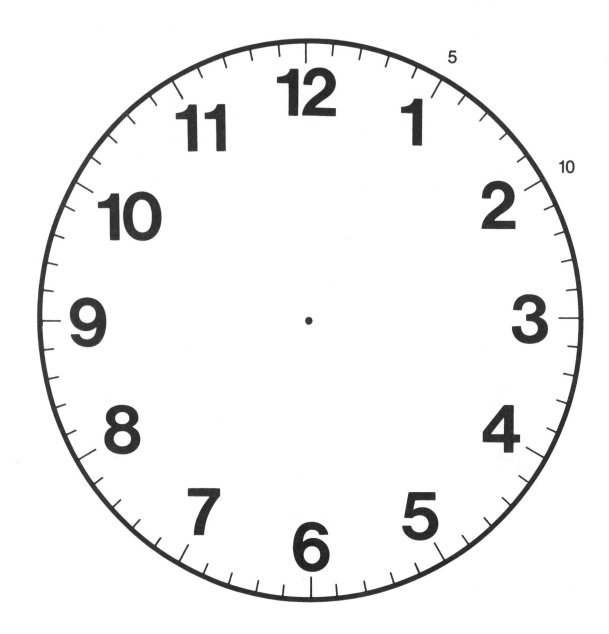

FIVE, TEN, FIFTEEN, TWENTY . . .

When minutes pass in an hour, we say the time as either *minutes after* or *minutes past*. When 60 minutes have passed, it is the next hour and the minute hand once again points to the 12.

Look at the clock faces below. The number of minutes that have passed in the hour are shown under each clock face. Draw the minute hands to show that these minutes have passed. The first one is done for you.

5 minutes **after**   10 minutes **past**   15 minutes **past**

25 minutes **past**   30 minutes **after**   40 minutes **after**

45 minutes **past**   55 minutes **after**   60 minutes **past**

WHERE DOES THE MINUTE HAND GO

Remember that digital clocks do not have hour or minute hands. Instead, the position of the numerals tells what the hour is and how many minutes have passed. For example, 10:25 shows that the hour the clock is telling about is 10 because the 10 comes before the colon. The numerals after the colon tell the minutes that have passed. In this example, 25 minutes have passed.

shows the hour the clock is telling about — **10:25** — *shows how many minutes have passed in the hour*

Draw the missing minute hands to show the same times on the round clock faces as the digital clock faces under them. The first one is done for you.

9:35   4:15   7:50

3:20   1:45   6:50

2:30   4:25   6:55

50

COUNTING AHEAD

To add minutes to a time already shown, first look at where the minute hand is. Then add the minutes to that point. For example, put your finger on the minute hand in the first exercise below. Look under that clock face to see how many minutes to add. This clock face needs 45 minutes added. Starting where the minute hand is, count by fives as you move your finger clockwise until you have counted 45 minutes. Then trace where the new minute hand belongs. Keep in mind that the more minutes the minute hand shows passing, the closer the hour hand gets to the next numeral. Now trace where the new hour hand belongs.

In the same way, draw the clock hands in the rest of the examples by yourself.

45 minutes   **30** minutes   **10** minutes

15 minutes   **20** minutes   **30** minutes

25 minutes   **50** minutes   **5** minutes

TIME TO THINK

Use your clock face to help you answer the following word problems.

1. Jan gets up at 7:15 every morning. She needs 45 minutes to get ready for school. What time does she leave her house to go to school? _____

2. It used to take Carlos 30 minutes to swim one mile. He has been practicing all week and now it takes him 5 minutes less. How many minutes does it take Carlos to swim one mile now? _____

3. Jean spent 20 minutes fixing her bike, 15 minutes washing it, and 10 minutes riding it. How much time did Jean spend with her bike? _____

4. Steve left his house at 1:00 P.M. He talked to his friend for 10 minutes, took 5 minutes to walk to his grandmother's house, played with her dog for 15 minutes, then rang her doorbell. What time was it when Steve rang his grandmother's doorbell? _____

5. Martin and his father painted Martin's clubhouse. They finished at 2:30 P.M. It took one hour for the paint to dry. What time was it when the paint dried? _____

6. Nancy put a cake in the oven at 3:00 P.M. It took 1 hour and 15 minutes to bake. What time was the cake ready? _____

COUNTING EVERY MINUTE

Digital and round clock faces both show how many minutes have passed in an hour. Digital clock faces change one minute at a time. It is easy to find how many minutes have passed on a digital clock face by looking where the minutes are shown, after the colon. A clock face showing 2:48 means 48 minutes have passed since the clock struck 2 o'clock.

To find exactly how many minutes have passed on a round clock face, count every line the minute hand has passed. Or, if the minute hand has moved far around the clock face, count by fives until no more groups of five are left. Because every line stands for one minute, count the rest of the lines up to where the minute hand is and add them to the first number you counted. For example, in the first exercise below, count clockwise by fives until you reach 45. The minute hand is 3 lines past where the line showing 45 minutes is, so add 3 plus 45. This means that 48 minutes have passed since the clock struck 2 o'clock.

Look at the remaining clock faces and fill in the missing minutes in the blanks under them.

2:48

10:_____

9:_____

6:_____

1:_____

12:_____

3:_____

11:_____

8:_____

53

SCHOOL TIME

 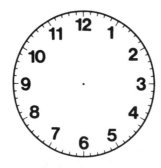 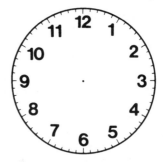

1. Draw the clock hands to show what time you start school.

2. Draw the clock hand to show the time you go to lunch.

3. Draw the clock hands to show what time your school day ends.

How many hours and minutes are you in school? _____

WHAT IS YOUR SCHOOL DAY LIKE?

Write your school activities for one day in order on the chart below.

Fill in the time each activity begins and ends.

Figure out how long each activity takes.

Activity	Start	Finish	Length
Example:			
1. Attendance taking	9:00 A.M.	9:15 A.M.	15 minutes
2.			
3.			
4.			
5.			
6.			
7.			
8.			

TIME GOES BY

Sometimes when minutes are added to a time they bring the time to the next hour. This happens when the added minutes go past the 60 minutes an hour has.

For example, if a clock face shows 4:55 it means 55 of the hour's 60 minutes have passed. If 5 minutes are added to that time, the new time is 5:00.

In the first example below, the time is 4:55 and 10 minutes are added. The new time is 5:00 plus 5 minutes, or 5:05. This happens because 55 minutes plus 10 minutes equals 65 minutes. An hour can only have 60 minutes, so the new hour is 5:00 plus 5 minutes. Put your finger on the minute hand and count ahead 10 minutes. Then trace the new clock hands and time.

Remember, the more minutes a minute hand shows passing, the closer the hour hand gets to the next numeral.

Look at each clock. Add the minutes given under each one, draw the new clock hands, and write the new times.

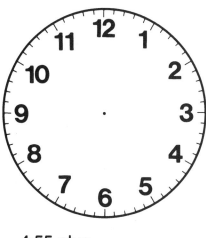

4:55 plus
10 minutes=_____

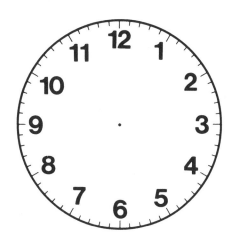

7:52 plus
5 minutes=_____

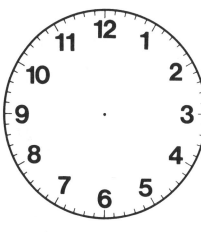

1:45 plus
30 minutes=_____

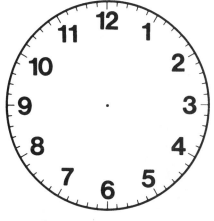

9:43 plus
25 minutes=_____

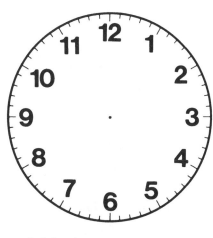

6:02 plus
17 minutes=_____

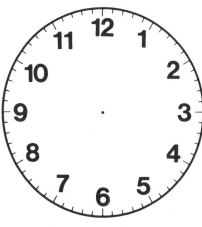

3:20 plus
45 minutes=_____

HOW LONG DOES IT TAKE?

Read the activities listed below. How long do you think it takes to do each one? Write your guesses on the chart and add your own activities, if you like. Then do them as you time yourself. Record how long the activities really take and compare these times to your guesses.

ACTIVITY	YOUR GUESS	ACTUAL TIME
1. Read your favorite poem.	_____	_____
2. Count to 100.	_____	_____
3. Draw a picture of your classroom.	_____	_____
4. Say your name, address, and telephone number.	_____	_____
5. Write the alphabet backwards.	_____	_____
6. _____	_____	_____
7. _____	_____	_____
8. _____	_____	_____
9. _____	_____	_____
10. _____	_____	_____

HOW TIME IS WRITTEN

To be able to understand a written time, you must know what the positions of the numerals and letters mean.

<u> 1 </u> : <u> 25 </u> A.M. or P.M.

The numeral or numerals here show the hour the clock is telling about.

The numeral or numerals here tell how many minutes of the hour have passed.

These letters mean "in the morning."

These letters mean "in the afternoon, evening, or night."

EXERCISES

1. Draw a circle around the *minutes* of the times below.

2. Mark an **X** on the *hours* of the times.

3. Write *A.M.* next to the times that say (morning).

4. Write *P.M.* next to the times that say (afternoon), (evening), or (night).

EXAMPLE   X̶:(25) <u>A.M.</u>   (morning)

3:21 _____ (afternoon)   9:15 _____ (night)

7:00 _____ (morning)   12:40 _____ (afternoon)

4:50 _____ (afternoon)   10:00 _____ (morning)

6:02 _____ (morning)   8:59 _____ (morning)

11:30 _____ (morning)   6:45 _____ (evening)

BEFORE AND AFTER THE HOUR

Imagine that the way the minute hand moves around the clock is like your trip to school. You start from your home (the 12 on the clock face) and go *to* school (the 6 on the clock face). Then you leave school and go *back* home.

Your trip is divided into two parts. The clock face can also be divided into two parts.

HOME

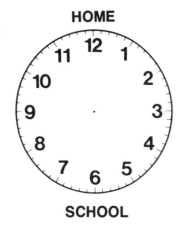

SCHOOL

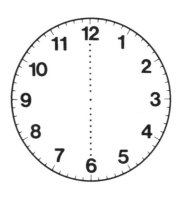

When the minute hand travels from the 12 to the 6, it tells the minutes that are *after* or *past* the hour. When it travels from the 6 back to the 12, it tells the minutes *before* or *to* the next hour.

Each of these parts is half of an hour, or 30 minutes. When the two parts are put together they equal one hour, or 60 minutes.

When people read time, they often say the time is "20 minutes *after* or *past* the hour." They also say "10 minutes *before* or *to* the hour."

Color the sides of these clock faces that the times describe.

5 minutes *after*

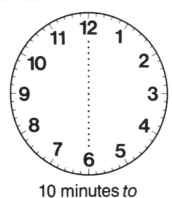

10 minutes *to*

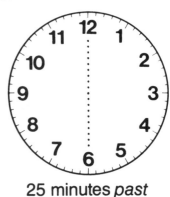

25 minutes *past*

COUNTING BEFORE THE HOUR

Find out how many mintues are "before the hour" by counting backward. Start at the 12 and stop just before you reach the 6. Write a numeral next to each line. The counting has already been started for you. Save this clock for the next activity.

WRITING TIME IN DIFFERENT WAYS

Read each time given below, then write the same times using the words *before, to, after,* or *past.* Use your clock face from the previous activity if you need help. The first example on each side is done for you.

before or **to** the hour	**after** or **past** the hour
1. **6:40** 20 minutes before 7:00 or 20 minutes to 7:00	1. **12:05** 5 minutes after 12:00 o r 5 minutes past 12:00
2. **2:31** _____ or _____	2. **4:13** _____ or _____
3. **8:56** _____ or _____	3. **10:17** _____ or _____
4. **7:45** _____ or _____	4. **6:23** _____ or _____
5. **5:50** _____ or _____	5. **11:29** _____ or _____

WORKING AROUND THE CLOCK

Look at the clock face below. There are spaces around the clock face with numerals showing how many minutes have passed at each point. Use these spaces and numerals to do the following activities.

ACTIVITIES

1. Color the spaces showing 20 minutes *after* the hour red.

2. Color the spaces showing 20 minutes *before* the hour blue.

3. Mark an **X** over the numeral that is *half way* around the clock face.

4. Draw circles in the space showing 5 minutes *past* the hour.

5. Draw circles in the space showing 5 minutes *to* the hour.

6. Circle the numeral that tells how many minutes are in one hour.

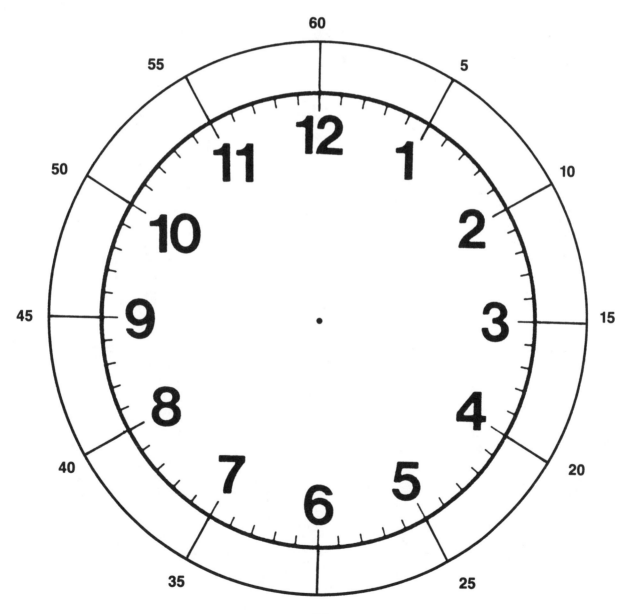

CLOCK LOTTO

PREPARATION

Photocopy the clock face below and the following game-piece page. Distribute one clock face to each child. Pair the students and give one game-piece page to each pair so that children may cut out the circles.

PLAY THE GAME

Partners place the game pieces face down. Then they alternate drawing one piece at a time and putting the piece on their clock face in the appropriate circle. If a piece is drawn for a circle that has already been filled, the piece is returned to the game-piece pile face down and the next child's turn begins. Explain that the numeral 12 is on everyone's clock face and that this circle does not need to be filled. The first partner to fill all the circles on his or her clock face wins.

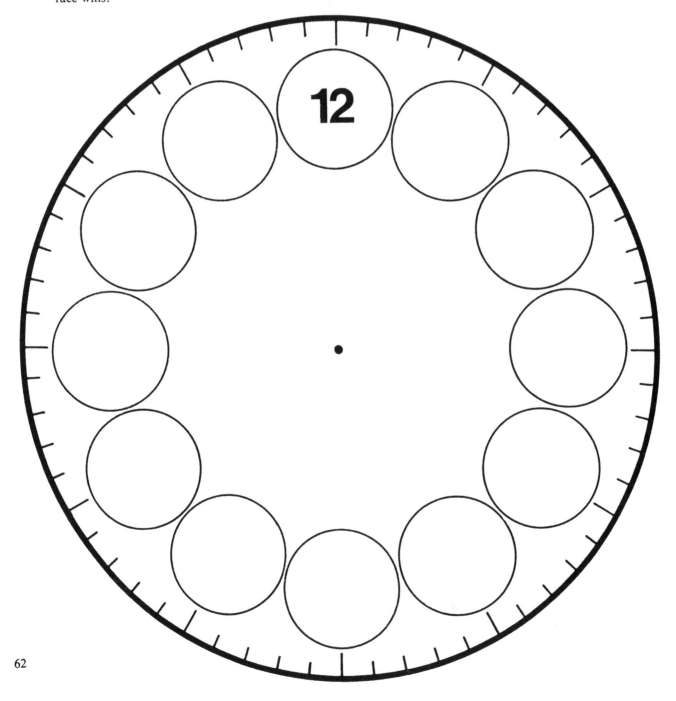

CLOCK LOTTO GAME PIECES

Cut out the game pieces below to play *Clock Lotto.*

5 after	10 to	half past	25 after	quarter before
25 past	5 before	20 after	quarter to	quarter past
20 before	quarter after	half hour before	20 to	25 before
10 past	10 before	5 to	25 to	10 after
	5 past	20 past		

ONE MORE TIME

EXTRA FOR EXPERTS:

Before you begin working on this page, write down the time._____

How long did it take you to complete this page? _____

Match the following times:

30 minutes after 6	12:00
quarter after 4	2:35
noon	12:15
half past 8	4:45
10 minutes before 11	7:45
25 minutes to 3	6:30
15 minutes past 1	4:15
quarter after 12	10:50
45 minutes after 7	8:30
quarter before 5	1:15

Fill in the digital clock face with the times below:

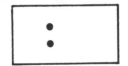

3 minutes after midnight

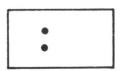

5 minutes to 6

Draw lines from the clock face to the matching time.

15 minutes past 2

8:45

quarter to 9

quarter after 2

1. **Jim was invited to a party that began at 2:30 P.M. He arrived at 2:00 P.M. How early was Jim?** _____

2. **Sarah went to a picnic at 4:00 P.M. She stayed until 5:15 P.M. How long did she stay?**_____

3. **It is now 1:00 P.M. Merissa must take her medicine at 3:30 P.M. How long will Merissa wait until she takes her medicine?**_____

4. **Patty arrives at school at a quarter after 8. She eats lunch at a quarter past 11. How many hours long is her morning at school?**_____